How Are They Made?
Sneakers

Wendy Blaxland

 **Marshall Cavendish**
Benchmark

New York

This edition first published in 2009 in the United States of America by Marshall Cavendish Benchmark.

Marshall Cavendish Benchmark
99 White Plains Road
Tarrytown, NY 10591
www.marshallcavendish.us

First published in 2008 by
Macmillan Education Australia Pty Ltd
15–19 Claremont Street, South Yarra 3141

Visit our website at www.macmillan.com.au or go directly to www.macmillanlibrary.com.au

Associated companies and representatives throughout the world.

Library of Congress Cataloging-in-Publication Data

Blaxland, Wendy.
   Sneakers / Wendy Blaxland.
      p. cm. -- (How are they made?)
   Includes index.
   ISBN 978-0-7614-3810-6
   1. Sneakers--Juvenile literature. I. Title.
   TS1910.B45 2008
   685'.3--dc22
                                 2008026211

4904

Edited by Anna Fern
Cover design, text design, and page layout by Cristina Neri, Canary Graphic Design
Photo research by Legend Images
Map by Damien Demaj, DEMAP; modified by Cristina Neri, Canary Graphic Design

Printed in the United States

Acknowledgments
The author would like to thank the following people for their expert advice: Jazz Bonifacio, footwear designer; Patrizia Mascianà, Statistics, Trade and Markets Division, F.A.O.; and Felicity Prentice, Lecturer, Department of Podiatry, La Trobe University, Australia.

The author and the publisher are grateful to the following for permission to reproduce copyright material:

Front cover photograph: Sneakers (left) © Alexander Kalina/iStockphoto; sneakers (right) © Jill Fromer/iStockphoto. Images repeated throughout title.

Photos courtesy of:
© adidas, **7**, **8**, **24**; Lee Jin-Man/AFP/Getty Images, **20** (left), **26** (bottom); Mark Ralston/AFP/Getty Images, **18**; Vicky Kasala/Digital Vision/Getty Images, **30** (right); Nathaniel S. Butler/NBAE via Getty Images, **27**; Spencer Platt/Getty Images, **28**; Forrest Anderson/Time Life Pictures/Getty Images, **21**, **22**; Andrew Holbrooke/Time Life Pictures/Getty Images, **16**; © Omar Ariff/iStockphoto, **14**; © Thomas Brostrom/iStockphoto, **11**; © Oscar Calero/iStockphoto, **4** (left); © Jeff Driver/ iStockphoto, **5** (top); © Rich Legg/iStockphoto, **5** (center); © Bruno Medley/iStockphoto, **10**; © Rhoberazzi/iStockphoto, **9**; © Jonathan Werve/iStockphoto, **5** (bottom); Photolibrary/Corbis, **19**; Photolibrary © Indiapicture/Alamy, **17**; Photos.com, **23** (top); © Stuart Taylor/Shutterstock, **4** (right); Sneaker Pimps, **25** (top); University of Connecticut, EcoHusky, **29** (top).

Headshot illustrations accompanying textboxes throughout title © Russell Tate/iStockphoto

1 3 5 6 4 2

Contents

Glossary Words

When a word is printed in **bold**, you can look up its meaning in the Glossary on page 31.

From Raw Materials to Products

Everything we use is made from raw materials from Earth. These are called natural resources. People take natural resources and make them into useful products.

Sneakers

Sneakers are very popular casual shoes originally designed for sports and other physical activities. They are different in style and build from dress shoes because they are made from flexible material and their soles are usually rubber.

The main raw materials used to make sneakers are plastic and rubber. Plastics are made from **petrochemicals**. Rubber is made from the sap of particular trees.

Leather, fabric, cements, and glues are also used to make sneakers. Leather is made from the skins of animals. Fabric is made from **natural fibers** or **synthetic fibers**. Cements and glues are made from chemicals.

Some sneakers are designed especially for skateboarders.

A sticky sap, called latex, is drained from trees to make the rubber for sneakers.

Most sneakers have shoelaces.

Sneakers with white soles are designed not to leave marks on special playing surfaces.

Why Do We Need Sneakers?

Sneakers protect feet and make walking and playing sports easier. Special types of sneakers are made for different sports. Most sneakers are worn for everyday use and are fashion statements as well as practical shoes.

Sneakers come in a huge range of styles, and can be cheap or very expensive. Twice as many sneakers are sold as other sorts of shoes.

Guess What!

Sneakers are called "felony shoes" in some parts of the world because they help criminals run away quickly. (A felony is a crime.) In one burglary in the United States, however, the police caught the suspect easily as he ran away across an open field in the dark. He was wearing sneakers with flashing lights!

Sneakers with cleats, or studs, are designed for running on grass playing fields.

The History of Sneakers

Shoes have been used for a very long time. Specialist sports shoes, however, developed in the 1800s. Then sneakers developed into a fashion item.

Sneakers through the Ages

700 BCE   The Greeks run races barefoot. They begin using shoes held on by strips of leather after their competitors win using them.

1830s   "Sandshoes" are made by Dunlop Rubber in the United Kingdom.

1875   The word "sneaker" is first used for a **croquet** shoe developed in the United States.

1860s   Special cycling shoes without heels are developed because of the new worldwide boom in riding bicycles.

Late 1800s   Rubber-soled shoes called plimsolls are developed in England.

1890s Studs are first used to make football cleats.

700 BCE   1 CE   1800   1820   1840   1860   1880

1790   Shoelaces are invented, made of string threaded through special holes made in shoes.

1840s   A method of hardening rubber and stopping it from decaying, called vulcanization, is developed at the same time in both the United States and England.

Late 1890s A British company now known as Reebok develops the earliest known spiked leather running shoes.

The modern company Adidas got its name from its founder, Adi Dassler.

Who is the patron saint of shoemakers?

The **patron saint** of shoemakers is Saint Crispin, a wealthy Roman who was persecuted for being a Christian. He and his brother fled to France where they made shoes for the poor. They survived drowning and being thrown into cauldrons of boiling lead and oil. October 25 is Saint Crispin's day, and was once a shoemaker's holiday.

1925 A German named Adi Dassler begins making running shoes.

1950s Sneakers are linked with the new teenage market and stand for going against the rules.

1930s Nylon is developed.

1908 The athletic shoe company Converse is founded in Massachusetts.

1976 Sponsorship, where athletes are paid to wear and **endorse** certain sneaker brands, is developed after a winning athlete at the Montreal Olympics is photographed giving credit to his running shoes.

1900

1920

1940

1960

1980

2000

1917 The name "sneakers" is first used to sell canvas-topped Keds (rhyming slang for ped, the Latin for "foot") made by the firm U.S. Rubber.

1950 Companies supply famous runners with free shoes in return for publicity about their sneakers.

1962 Scientifically tested shoes are developed.

1970s Herbert Lapidus invents odor-eater insoles with charcoal to absorb odors because his wife has very smelly feet.

What Are Sneakers Made From?

The uppers of sneakers may be made of canvas or synthetic fabric, leather, or more likely a combination of these. The soles are generally made of plastic materials and rubber. Sneakers are held together by cement or **resin**.

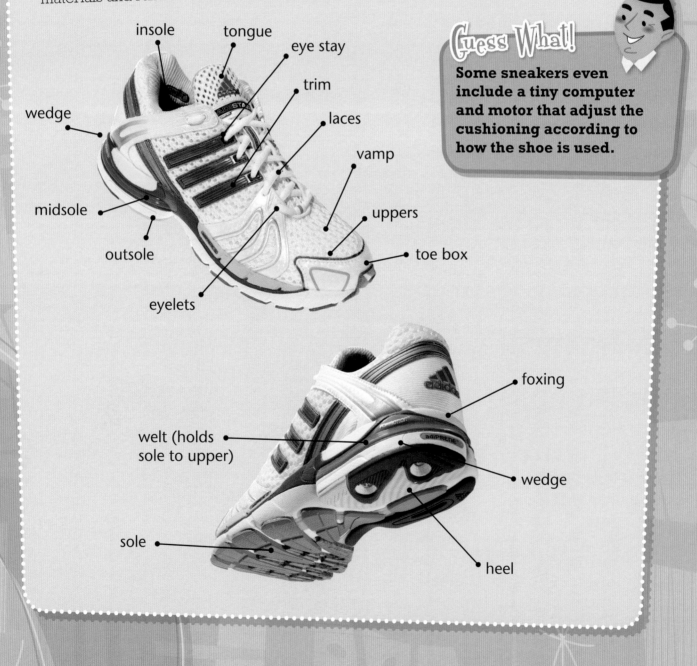

insole
tongue
eye stay
trim
laces
vamp
uppers
toe box
eyelets
wedge
midsole
outsole

Guess What!

Some sneakers even include a tiny computer and motor that adjust the cushioning according to how the shoe is used.

foxing
welt (holds sole to upper)
wedge
sole
heel

8

Materials

A surprising variety of raw materials is used in sneakers. As with the making of all products, energy is also used to run the machines that mine and harvest the raw materials, make the leather and cloth, and assemble and decorate the sneakers.

Materials Used to Make Sneakers

Material	Purpose and Qualities
Canvas	Used for the uppers, this fabric lets feet breathe.
Leather or synthetic leather	Used for the uppers and shoelaces, these materials are flexible and strong.
Synthetic fabric	Used for the uppers and shoelaces, this is light, cheap, and durable.
Mesh	Used for the uppers, mesh lets feet breathe.
Plastic	Used for uppers, soles, and laces, plastic is cheap, light, flexible, and cushions feet.
Rubber	Used in the outsoles, rubber is flexible and cushions feet.
Resins, cements	Hold the soles and uppers of sneakers together.
Metal	Used for the aglets, the ends of shoelaces that make them easy to thread.
Dyes	Used to color the sneakers and make them attractive.
Thread	Used to stitch parts of the uppers together.
Trim	Trim made from different material may decorate the uppers and make them look special.

Guess What!

The term sole derives from *solea*, a Latin word meaning soil or ground.

Sneaker soles are made from tough material to protect the feet.

Sneaker Design

Sneaker designs change rapidly, and styles are often sold only for a short time. Sneaker **manufacturers** compete to show their sneakers as new, better, and more fashionable. Manufacturers identify their sneakers by a **logo** on each sneaker that instantly advertises the firm. For example, Nike sneakers are easily recognizable by the "swoosh" design that decorates every pair.

Sneaker designers work very closely with the firm's master shoemaker, who knows what can be made and how, to arrive at a final design.

Shoes are designed around human feet. Every foot is different, and 90 percent of people have feet of different sizes. Designers need to take many different foot measurements to make sure people will be able to wear their designs comfortably.

Sneaker designers use a number of different materials and techniques.

Design Influences

Designers are always trying to come up with new and better sneakers. Designs are influenced by the latest information about how the body moves and by newly developed materials.

Foot-care specialists, called podiatrists, also influence sneaker design. They look at the health of feet, the way feet move, and the needs of athletes. Podiatric improvements to sneakers include arch supports and heel cradles. Space research has also helped design better sneakers, for instance, to improve air flow.

The design of the outer sole of sneakers helps them grip the ground. It is also part of the overall sneaker design. Early sole patterns were circles and squares, then herringbones and grid squares. Now, the sole pattern usually includes the designer's logo.

Question & Answer

What are "kangaroos" and "skunks"?

"Kangaroos" were sneakers with a pocket made in the mid-1980s. Black Converse were nicknamed "Skunks." The 1970s canvas track-training shoes had a white stripe on the back like a tail.

Soles eventually wear out because they rub against the ground at every step.

From Leather and Rubber to Sneakers

The process of making everyday objects such as sneakers from raw materials involves a large number of steps. In the first stage, the leather and rubber are prepared. The second stage consists of making the sole and sneaker upper. The sole consists of different layers of rubber and plastic made separately. The sneaker upper is made from shaped and decorated pieces of leather and other materials. In the final stage, the sneakers are assembled. The uppers are stitched together and formed into the right shape around a plastic **mold** called a last. Then, the inner sole is stitched to the upper. Next, the midsole and outer soles are glued on before the sneaker is trimmed and finished with laces or fasteners.

Stage Two:

Stage One: Making Sneaker Materials

Latex is collected from rubber trees.	The skins of animals are cleaned.
⬇	⬇
Then the latex is heated with chemicals to make it into strong and elastic rubber.	Next, they are soaked in chemicals to make them flexible and **waterproof**. This is called tanning.

Other materials, such as plastic and canvas cloth, may also be used to make sneakers.

Stage Three: Assembling the Sneakers

First, the pieces of leather for the upper are stitched or glued together.

↓

Then the upper is fitted around a plastic mold, called a last, to form the shape of the shoe.

↓

Next, the inner layer of the sole is stitched or glued to the upper.

↓

After this, the heel and toe box are stiffened.

↓

Then, the rubber sole is glued to the upper.

↓

Finally, the sneaker is finished with shoelaces or fasteners and any decorative trims.

Making Sneaker Parts

The soles of sneakers have different layers made in different ways.

The outer sole is made by squeezing liquid rubber through a hole into a mold of the right shape and heating it to harden it.

↓

The insole is made of thin, foamy, molded plastic that is also hardened by heating.

↓

The midsole, which cushions the foot, is usually made of tough polyurethane plastic. It contains materials such as gel, silicone, or compressed air.

The leather and other materials are cut into shaped pieces to make the upper.

↓

Then these pieces may be decorated with colored dyes, printed patterns, or by having holes punched into them.

Question & Answer

What is "sneakerjacking"?

Sneakerjacking is being held up by someone who wants to steal your (usually expensive) sneakers! The term follows words such as hijacking and carjacking.

13

Raw Materials for Sneakers

Making sneakers brings together materials from animals, plants, and minerals from all over the world.

Leather is produced from animal skins in a wide range of countries. Fifty-five percent of leather produced is used in making shoes, though not necessarily sneakers.

Natural rubber is a gum produced by a tree grown in the **tropics**. The three largest rubber-producing countries, Indonesia, Malaysia, and Thailand, together account for around 72 percent of all natural rubber production. More than half of the world's rubber is now produced synthetically.

The plastics used in sneakers all come from oil and gas produced by the petrochemical industry. The largest petrochemical industries are found in the United States and Western Europe. New facilities, however, are mainly in the Middle East and Asia.

Oil, often extracted from under the sea floor by oil rigs, is the raw material used to make plastic.

ARCTIC OCEAN

NORTH AMERICA
* United States of America

PACIFIC OCEAN

ANTARCTIC OCEAN

Centers for Sneaker Production

Sneakers are made in many countries. The four major manufacturing countries, however, are in Asia, and the next five in Europe.

Key

- ✪ Important rubber-producing countries
- ◆ Important leather-producing countries
- ☀ Important oil-producing countries
- 👟 Important sneaker-manufacturing countries

This map shows countries that are important to the production of sneakers.

Stage One: Making Sneaker Materials

The main parts of sneakers are the uppers, made from leather, and the soles, made from rubber. Many other materials, especially plastics, may also be used in sneaker uppers and soles.

Rubber

Natural rubber comes from latex, a gum collected from tropical **plantations** of rubber trees. Workers make a shallow cut in the bark and leave a small cup to collect the oozing gum. The rubber is heated with other substances, such as sulfur, to make it harder and more elastic and to stop it decaying. This is called vulcanization. Synthetic rubber is made from chemicals in factories.

These women are assembling rubber sneaker soles.

Question & Answer

What is the best way to clean and dry sneakers?

To clean sneakers, keep them out of the washing machine. Use a damp cloth and mild soap, baby wipes, or an old toothbrush. Some sneaker fans swear by electric toothbrushes! To dry them, take out the shoelaces and put them in a warm, airy place, but don't use a clothes dryer.

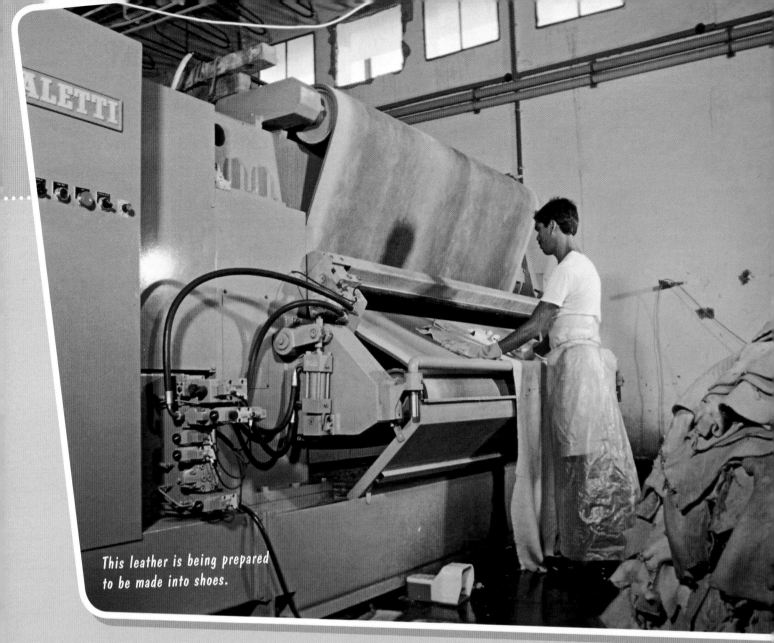

This leather is being prepared to be made into shoes.

Leather

Leather is made from the skins of animals, mainly cattle. The process of turning the skins into leather is called tanning.

The skins are first cleaned and salted to stop them from rotting. They are then tanned, which involves soaking the skins in special chemicals called tannins. Tanning is done either with metal or vegetable tannins and can take up to a year. This process makes the leather flexible and waterproof.

After tanning, the leather is washed, split to the right thickness, oiled, and dyed. It is then stretched and dried.

Finally, the leather is brushed and polished, ready to be sent to the sneaker factory.

Question & Answer

What are "tackies," "bubblegums," and "plimsolls"?

Sneakers! "Tackies" is a South African term for sneakers and tires. "Bubblegums" is 1970s Californian slang for cheap, no-name sneakers. "Plimsolls" are old-fashioned British canvas sneakers. Sneakers are also called "kicks," "trainers," "runners," and "sandshoes."

Stage Two: Making Sneaker Parts

The two main parts of a sneaker are the upper and the sole.

Making the Uppers

First, the pieces of leather for the sneaker uppers are cut out. This may be done by laser, or with sharp, steel cutting tools called **dies**, which stamp out pieces like cookie cutters.

The leather and other materials can be dyed different colors, printed with patterns, punched with holes, or decorated in other ways. The pattern pieces are arranged carefully on the leather to avoid wasting any.

Question & Answer

How many times do a pair of sneakered feet hit the ground when an adult runs 1 mile (1.6 kilometers)?

An adult's sneakered feet hit the ground 795 times every mile.

A factory worker prepares pieces of leather for shoes.

This machine is molding soles with studs in them for sports shoes.

Making the Soles

The soles of sneakers are made separately. They have a number of layers, depending on the design. Normally there are three layers: the insole, midsole, and outsole.

The insole is usually a thin layer of white, foamy plastic called E.V.A. (ethylene vinyl acetate), which may be cut out or molded. The midsole provides most of the cushioning. Generally it is made of polyurethane, a tough and often flexible plastic. This surrounds softer gel, liquid silicone, polyurethane foam, or capsules of compressed air. The midsoles are also molded or cut by dies. The outsole is normally made of rubber, either die-cut or molded.

Rubber and plastics are generally made into the correct shape by transfer molding. In this process, the material is squeezed through a hole into a mold and heated to harden it.

Question & Answer

Which gases are used in air-cushioned shoes?

The gases helium and nitrogen have both been used by different manufacturers. At least four manufacturers use air-cushioned soles.

Stage Three: Assembling the Sneakers

A sneaker may have as many as twenty parts to it. Assembling these pieces is skilled work.

The pieces that will form the upper are first stitched or glued together and the holes for the shoelaces are punched out. The upper now looks not like a shoe, but like a round hat.

The upper is heated and fitted around a plastic mold called a last, which forms the final shape of the shoe. The extra material in the uppers, called the lasting margin, will be folded underneath the shoe when it is cemented to the sole. Any other details, such as patterns of holes and labels, are now added.

Next, the insole is stitched to the sides of the upper, cemented to it, or inserted. The heel and toe box are stiffened with extra material.

Then, the different layers of the midsole, which cushion the foot, are bonded together and cemented to the outer sole.

Finally, the upper and sole are glued together.

A sock liner made of fabric may be put inside the shoe to protect the sole.

These workers are assembling sneaker uppers.

These sneakers are ready to have laces threaded into them and other finishing touches.

Finishing the Sneakers

Once the sneaker is assembled, any extra glue needs to be trimmed. Special workers called singers (sin-jers) burn off any loose threads.

Polishers stain, wax, polish, or brush the leather according to the design of the sneakers. Other workers add laces and labels. Fastenings, such as **Velcro**, or even a zipper are added.

Once the shoe is complete, an inspector checks for problems with lasting, stitching, and cementing.

Question & Answer

What is an "aglet"?

An aglet is the metal, plastic, or fiber tube tip that stiffens the end of shoelaces to let you lace them.

Packaging and Distribution

Products are packaged to protect them while they are being transported. Packaging also displays the maker's brand and makes products look attractive when they are sold.

Sneakers are packaged in different ways. The cheapest sneakers are sold without any packaging. Most sneakers are sold in shoe boxes showing the maker's special logo or colors, as well as the model and size. They are usually wrapped in tissue paper to protect them, and may be stuffed with tissue paper to keep their shape. Little packets with chemicals keep the sneakers dry.

Designer or limited edition sneakers may have specially designed boxes. Companies even hire graffiti artists to decorate boxes for special models. Really special boxes may include certificates of authenticity or cleaning brushes.

Guess What!

Sneakers still in their original boxes are worth much more to collectors. Some collectors even shrink-wrap their sneakers to keep them in mint or top condition. Sneakers that have never been tried on or even removed from their packaging are called "dead stock."

These sneakers are being packed into boxes at a shoe factory in Shenzen, China.

Choosing which sneakers suit you best can be an important decision.

Distribution

Sneakers are often made in one country and sold in others. To transport them to where they will be sold, they are packed together in cartons, which are loaded into identical shipping containers. The shipping containers travel on trains or trucks, then on ships between countries.

Sneakers are sent from factories in large quantities to **wholesalers**. They are then stored in warehouses and distributed in smaller numbers, usually by truck, to the stores that sell them.

Retail outlets for sneakers include department stores, chain stores, general shoe stores, specialist sneaker stores, and exclusive boutiques for the most expensive sneakers.

Sneakers are also sold on the Internet directly by the companies that make or distribute them. Hard-to-get or exclusive sneakers may be sold on auction sites such as eBay.

Marketing and Advertising

Marketing and advertising are used to promote and sell products.

Marketing

More sneakers are sold than any other sort of shoes, and companies spend a lot of money promoting them.

One major selling point for sneakers is rarity. Producing limited numbers of a design makes them prized. One store in the United States had to let customers who had just bought the new Nike Pigeon Dunk sneakers out the back way to avoid fights with other disappointed buyers.

Another sales technique from big companies is letting people design their own sneakers. One-of-a-kind "kicks" by young, underground shoe designers and graffiti artists can be very expensive.

Some companies stress their environmental values as a selling point. For example, Blackspot sneakers have been produced without using animal products or exploiting workers.

Basketball star Gilbert Arenas appears in advertisements for Adidas sneakers.

Question & Answer

How many sneaker companies did the Dassler family found?

At least three. Adi Dassler started Adidas, while his brother Rudolf started Puma. Later on, a grandson of Adi Dassler (also named Adi Dassler) started the sneaker company A.D. One.

These one-of-a-kind Nintendo Nikes are part of the Sneaker Pimps exhibition.

Advertising

Sneakers are advertised everywhere, from magazines, television, and radio ads to websites. The Internet has fueled a marketing explosion from sneaker enthusiasts, too. A search engine called "Solepedia" (a sneaker encyclopedia!) lets **sneakerheads** explore online sneaker shops, auctions, and forums.

Advertisements often link sneakers with what's cool in youth culture. They pay celebrity sportspeople, such as Michael Jordan, and musicians, such as Eminem, to endorse sneakers.

The big companies stress the high-tech nature of their shoes and use sneaker testers (usually professional athletes) to test new styles. Companies sponsor sports events and organizations, too.

Guess What!

Peter Fahey, an Australian sneakerhead, has developed Sneaker Pimps, a traveling sneaker art exhibition, which has been displayed worldwide. It shows more than one thousand pairs of rare, **vintage**, and artist-designed sneakers and is sponsored by all the big sneaker companies.

Production of Sneakers

Products may be made in factories in huge quantities. This is called mass production. They can also be made in small quantities by hand, by skilled craftspeople.

Mass Production

Almost all sneakers are mass produced. Big companies make huge numbers of the same sort of sneaker. This reduces the cost of a single pair by spreading the cost of designing, making, and advertising them.

Wearing the same sort of sneakers makes people feel they belong to a group. People often develop a loyalty to a brand of sneakers and feel it guarantees certain qualities. Online petitions even try to persuade companies to bring back particular sneaker styles.

Factories, such as this one in South Korea, make huge numbers of sneakers.

Guess What!

One Nike factory in China, called "Shoetown," employs more than ten thousand people.

Sneaker companies sometimes produce one-of-a-kind designs for top athletes.

Small-scale Production

While people want to belong, they also want to feel unique. Nike reminds people that the company began with dedicated individuals when it tells the famous story of one of its cofounders, Bill Bowerman, pouring rubber into his wife's waffle iron to make soles for sneakers he was hand-building for athletes he coached.

Some people want to wear unusual or exclusive sneakers. Several big sneaker companies now have ways to let people design their own sneakers, and they employ top designers to create exclusive sneakers. There is also a growing trend towards one-of-a-kind pairs of sneakers hand-painted by artists.

Guess What!

Fake sneakers are made by copying well-known sneakers, with small changes to names or logos, and sold more cheaply. Fake brands include Recbuk, Nyke, and Jaguar (copying Reebok, Nike, and Puma). Big companies take people who make or sell fake brands to court for stealing their designs.

Sneakers and the Environment

Making any product affects the environment. It also has an effect on the people who make the product. It is important to think about the impact of a product through its entire life cycle. This includes getting the raw materials, making the product, and disposing of it. Any problems need to be worked on so products can be made in the best ways available.

Materials

Farming the rubber trees needed to make rubber and the cattle needed for leather has an environmental cost. Farmers use water, fertilizers, and pesticides, which all have an impact on the environment.

The processes of making rubber and leather and other materials for sneakers can also involve dangerous substances that may create pollution. Governments and industries work to reduce poisonous waste and watchdog organizations check on them.

Factory Working Conditions

The way some sneaker factories in developing countries treat their workers has drawn much attention worldwide. Concerns include children working in factories, low wages, long hours, and poor conditions. Consumer protests have encouraged large companies to take steps to improve conditions for their workers.

Consumer protests can help to improve working conditions in the sportswear industry.

You can find information on the Internet about sneaker recycling programs.

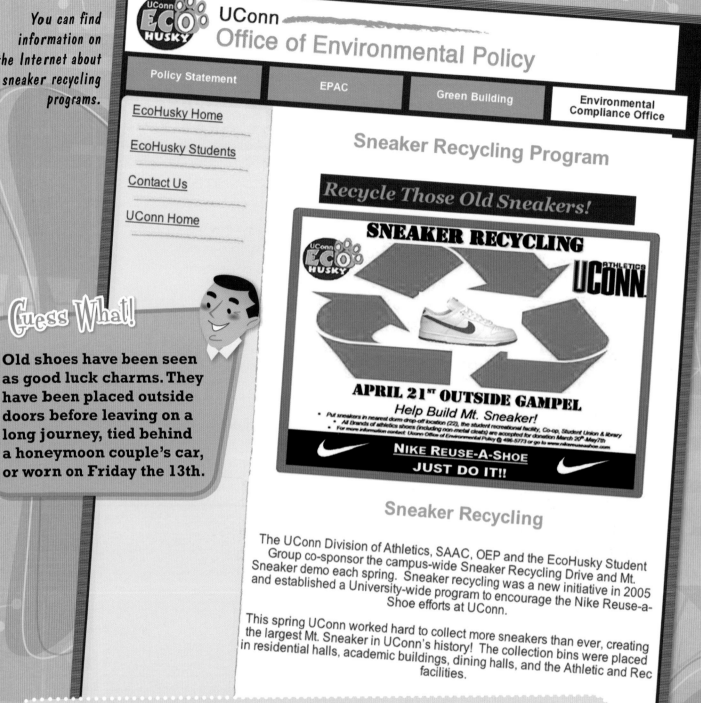

Recycling

Several large companies run programs to recycle old sneakers. The Nike Grind program separates sneakers into rubber from the outsoles, foam from the midsoles, and material from the uppers. These substances are separately ground into small lumps and then used to make surfaces such as running tracks, tennis courts, and padding under basketball floors.

Some plastics can be melted and reused. Those that cannot be reused may be burned to provide energy.

Index